No Games Allowed

Courtney LaNell

No Games Allowed

Belle Publishing
1742 NE 23rd St
Suite B
Oklahoma City, OK. 73111
www.bellepublishingllc.co
bellepublishingllc@gmail.com
Ordering Information:
Quantity sales. special discounts are available on quantity purchases by corporations, associations, and others. For details, contact the address above.

First Edition
ISBN- 978-1-953928-51-1

Table of Contents

Intro...

He said my pussy was dangerous
My walk an indication
of an entanglement
He requested 50ft; he wasn't signing
a release and he just knew what I was
working with was a liability

He almost offended me...

I offered a non-disclosure because I
needed him to know I don't play those
types of games

He's clearly been dealing with lames...

That shit clouded his judgment and I
keep trying to prove I'm not the same
I just want my pussy on his face,
grinding on his tongue, palms
applying pressure to hold his place

I'm not one to ask for what should
already be mine...but the chemistry...
it keeps me intrigued
I'll fall back though
and just wait my time...

Everything

He kissed my imperfections
As if he had the power to bless me
Looked me in my eyes and reassured
me, I was...everything
Spoke about how he needed me
without speaking a word to me
I felt safe in his space
Emotionally exposed before he even
had a chance to undress me

Guard down, eyes closed,
he received parts of me
I promised never
to set free
Clearly, I didn't learn my lesson...
I relaxed my thoughts...
Conceded to solicitation
Let go of inhibitions
And let him have his way with me

I let him fuck me like
he needed me...like
Like his side piece
Not because I was a secret
but because he needed peace
As much as me...

Deep breaths, long strokes,
a slight choke...

Definitely a practiced effort
A master at his craft

A creator of cunnilingus conquest
that can only be described as art

Abstract thoughts, filled with
opposition knowing the moment
he gets me
I become his victim

I surrender so he can save me
Deliver me from inadequacy
Calm an urgency
And reawaken an appreciation
For every flaw and curve that is me

This man is conscious of the
consideration from our creator to
design such a masterpiece
He takes his time and loves
every part of me
Delivering exactly what
he promised he'd be

From fellatio fantasies

exceeding expectations
and cunnilingus—allowing me
to leave my problems
in his beard

I'm grateful...

To bringing me to a revolutionary
level climax while speaking
affirmations to me

With each release, he poured into me
Used his tongue to speak life into me

This man manifested
my dreams with me

Told me I could be anything I
wanna be, while holding me

He knows my favorite
position is ascension

He taught me tantra with tools
blessed from the universe and skills
only meditation could bring

I'm grateful...

This vibration is beyond sexual

It's a catalyst toward my purpose

A gift from the universe
Demonstrating the power in pleasure
Sex is about more than
just cumin and gripping the sheets

He kissed my imperfections
As if he had the power to bless me

Looked me in my eyes and reassured
me I was...everything

Unhinged Vulnerability

He touched my soul today
Fingers gripping my weave and
I didn't even question his ways
His motives, his moves
I'm wit it
Everything he does points to pleasure
Pressure applied, each release better
No, not one moment without him
pleasing me above and beyond
some average lover
Each stroke is a reminder
I'm in the right place
Tears down my face, signaling a slow
explosion and lack of control
while he invades my space
I welcome his intrusion
A pleasant interruption from
basic and mundane

It was so good I called
and left a review
Put a 1 next to likely to recommend
Because I be damn
If I share this D with a stranger
or a friend
I'm normally not selfish

but I'm lying if they ask
I'ma tell em its trash

This dick is mine until I say it's not
I'm clocking in and out like I have
a quota to meet

You see..with this D I'm complete
I get to be me

Unhinged vulnerability...

No safe words needed
His piece is my peace
I return the favor and
become his freak

Using my skills on the stage, I go deep
and let him fuck me mentally...

Pushing the limits, my thoughts
dripping from his mic, amplifying my
desire to spit—all his favorite shit

He's a fan of mine and I'm a fan of his
I rate every performance a 10

Every time I cum it's just
a reason to come again

I don't know who told this man what I
needed but I'm grateful
they didn't keep it a secret

I took a chance so I could release
May be crazy to some but for me, this
is what I call Unhinged vulnerability...

Dear Diary.....

I'm optimistic when he licks it
because he knows exactly
what she's missing
He devours me like Uber Eats
in every position
So much so...
I diagnosed him with
a predisposed condition
You see...
His moves are familiar to me
Like Deja Vu
Like do you know me?
Do I know you?
I'm nervous as hell but I let him
continue his game
He played with my kitty until
she purred like a lion
Sucking my clit with an intent
that I recognized
I looked in his eyes as he
watched me reach for the sheets
His eyes...
I know them
He continued to work
His tongue game amazing as he
watched me watch him...pleasing me

I gripped his head, ignored my
thoughts and grinded until his beard
was covered in cream
He flipped me over and pressed his
hand in my back,
creating an arch but his left hand
never left his snack
His tongue was in my ass
before I could protest or say hold on
He played with my clit and ate his
snack from the back
All while, he whispered for me to cum
harder again and again
I gave in to his commands, but I
couldn't shake the feeling
that I knew this man
This gift he was giving way too good
not to recall the experience
Fuck it, I'll ask him
Maybe he'll remember it...
Just as I was about to
put myself out there,
and ask for help from my forgotten
one-night stand
My phone began to ring
on the nightstand
It read in capital letters
Johnny Overstreet
It was clearly lit up
And I know he could see

We once again made eye contact and
it all started coming back to me

He must have realized it too
because he smiled and licked his lips
Yet...he never said shit
I knew, that he knew, that I knew,
that I had smashed his dad...

His pops, his padre,
the source of his DNA...
I was conflicted...
But I no longer had to
question his skills
I now knew why he was an
expert in this field
Orgasm after orgasm,
he made me remember
These skills were inherited
Passed down from generations

And gifted to me
I whispered thank you to the
universe, reached for the phone
and said hello...

To Be Continued...

Flowered Fantasies

I want this forbidden fruit to make
you float, take you higher
than any strain
I need your concentration on this
hybrid while these chemicals
release pure intoxication

Let the flavor of this flower drip from
your lips and call your name
Taste my purple passion while you
sample my cookies on this
Pineapple Express

These cookies are potent, but I want
you to reach euphoria when you dip
your tongue in this mimosa

This pussy cums with a calming
hybrid punch and sativa dominant to
bring out your creativity

With fruitful fantasies and
flower dreams
Giving you relief as you
release dopamine

I'm a feen for you on every strain,

In every way

You stimulate every part of me
I feel you in my bloodstream
Paranoid and fatigued...I need you
inside of me

Appetite increased,
erratic thoughts exposed
Blue Mango, Strawberry kush
and Do si Dos

The aroma orgasmic, hypnotic
and pure
I'm focused on you and these
homegrown thoughts with a
top-shelf freak

Ready to drip like Skittles on a hot day
painting a rainbow on your lips

I'm the primary component
guaranteed to cure any affliction and
cause 100% addiction

Smoke me, please...

Written by: Souls InkPen

For Her

I wanted to buy a flower

I want to go to the most expensive boutique the city has to offer

For her

I wanna find myself asking questions I thought I'd never ask, like

Do I need to put this in a pot or will a vase do?

Could I plant it in the open for the world to see how much I love SHE and SHE could wake up smiling daily cause FINALLY she's able to see the beauty I see in her growing wildly

For her

I'd sift through pamphlets, talk to different plant heads, meet with

every flower lady possible, picking
petals of knowledge JUST....

Hoping to get it right

For her

I'd acquire a green thumb; learn the
ways of the Great Ones as if I were a
padowan

For her

I'd try...

My thumb just isn't that green and
therefore all plant life crumbles
around me and I'm assuming that's
the way it's meant to be based off
everything I've seen

Let me break it down for you

For her

I wasn't buying roses as they are
too often given

I wasn't buying carnations cause
there wasn't a burial nor was there
real cause for celebration

For her

I wasn't buying dandelions, daffodils
nor was I after star gazing lilies

For her

I was just trying to buy some weed

SEE, she likes the way it takes her
pain away even if for a little while and
I can't lie seeing her high is hella
hilarious cause her smile already
lights up rooms

But when she's on kush it lights up
ENTIRE STADIUMS

I grew up in the old adage
You can always do more with

"The More You Know"

So, when I sifted through those
pamphlets and spoke to those plant

heads I swiped a couple of those
seeds cause much like that weed

With her, I want to grow

I Said What I Said

Girls can never say they want it...
But I'm eager to speak
Speak about all the ways I hear him
calling for me
Inexperienced with this feeling but
craving it because it seems familiar
Dripping in apprehension with
a hunger to please
No longer cautious of my desires
and irrational fears
My body is yours
You're what I need
Do as you please...

He Loves Me

I love the way you love on her
the way your tongue fits like
a glove inside her
Her waterfall steady flowing,
lips moaning an inaudible melody
Singing praises to the Most High
for his creation

this man
this sexy
this chocolate
oh, man

Thank you for this man

searching deep
licking slow
sucking hard
gripping tight

oh, this man

This love he gives me makes my heart
race to my legs
and shake to my feet
His rigorous excavation
inside my walls
lights me on fire and cools my soul

I need this feeling this man gives me
in this moment to last
beyond this moment

I'm craving his love
his touch
his kiss
I need it all

With this man there are
no boundaries
I am his
He is mine
Oh, man
I love this man

Unqualified Applicant

It’s mandatory that this pussy be ate
in a manner that I'm accustomed to
In order for me to cum for you
Timid actions, a limited package and
no knowledge of the proper way to
perform cunnilingus?

He just down there playing and shit...

Contemplating on what he would do
if someone had taught him
a trick or two
Instead of pushing him aside when he
left them unsatisfied

Allow me to express myself in this
teachable moment...

You wouldn't recognize legs shaking
if you came eye to eye with Bambi
after he became an orphan in the
woods

Oh, ni**a, you just cocky for
no reason

You played me, talking that good shit
on a sunny day
Asking if this kitty wanna play
As if your toy would
hold her attention
You sold that shit to me like it
was a limited edition

You failed to realize you were dealing
with a woman this time
I tried to guide you but like a typical
man you chose not to listen

Just when I was in the right position
and your tongue finally found that
spot that your dumb ass kept missing
You lost all sense of direction

Ni**a, I would have voted for you
Told my girls, "oh, bihhh the stories
are true!"

Now I'm trying to figure out how to
finish the rest of the night
without you
You a fraud in the bedroom
and that shit is foul

I'm pulling your application
Hell, I'm shredding
your whole damn file

Lame Sex Game

Promises of fire head
fall on deaf ears
I'm immune to the tales
of your alleged skills
How you plan to make my back
bend and arch
And leave me calling to heaven
for a free thought
The neighbors will for sure ask who is
this man for which I speak in tongues
And I'll probably slide off the bed
after I cum

Blah blah blah...

Yes, I need all this you speak of
and more
But are you man enough to execute
all that you preach

Please don't expect a big freak
When you're still afraid to
clean your plate
I need you not to hesitate and sit
down to this table and eat

I want you so full we both fall asleep

This is a marathon and not a sprint
Pace yaself before you
end up in a poem
About a nigga who lacking, slacking
and lying about what he packin

Your lane is yours for a reason
Stay in it, cause this ride is for
a man who can hang
Respect my honesty cause I didn't
speak for no reason...

Step ya game up or get out my DMs
Cause I promise you over here,
I'm not letting nothing slide

Ladies, speak up, the truth is needed
We checking a ni**a lame sex game
all seasons

(Response to Unqualified Applicant)
Written by: Souls Ink Pen

Over-Qualified

She said something about some men not knowing how to perform cunnilingus...

Something about legs shaking and not knowing the difference

She said something about it having to be eaten in the way she was used to

But, baby girl, I'm here to remove all doubt as well as memories of the old school because my tongue knows no bounds, I'm not here to imprint on your mentals

I'm here to leave soulful bruises on you

Let me begin...

You're used to men talking a big game and not being able to back it up

You're used to men talking about how
they can do certain things and make
you scream but my goal is neither

I just want to make you have
recurring dreams—Wake up in a bed
soaking from nightmares of you
running

Hand-gripped sheets, toes curled,
legs parted beneath blankets as the
bed feels the anointed oils from your
cave of wonders as it seeps

Ironically, I haven't even
touched you yet...

Magically, I'm starting to see beads of
sweat because, let's face it, you know
me not to be a liar and to be brutally
honest with my truth, and one of the
things I pride myself in is being a
gamer and like Shang Tsung I'm going
to suck the soul from you

See these men out here love telling
stories about how they can beat the
pussy up but I'll never tell that lie
because I'll never gas myself up

I'll never tell you about how I can
rearrange your walls and I'll never tell
you about how I can do all types of
that other shit but what I will say is

You'll never be bored with me, I'm
something you'll never forget

Especially, when my lips meet the
nape of your neck, then slide slowly
down your spine

Kissing both of your cheeks as you
bend over in front of me then I start
sucking your clit from behind

I'll lead you to the bed, as I lick slowly
around the labia; there are sensitive
spots of the vagina on top, and watch
me wade and play in your still waters

Then I'll slide my fingers in, at half an
inch or I can slowly press on and
massage your string striking the
chord of "G"

But here you are talking all this shit
about what men can't do but now I've
got you wanting to...

Cum for me

I don't need your legs shaking like
Bambi, I don't need you telling your
girls about what I did

All I'll have to do is lift up my shirt and
they can see from all the scratches
that I'm the shit

They'll understand from your sudden
silence once they ask how your night
went and when your cheeks turn
rosy red as you think sweet laments

Yes, I said lament because you'll be
mad at yourself for not choosing me
as your forever, someone else will
end up with the prize but deep down
inside you'll know I'm the one who
done it better

They'll never kiss your feet as I did the
night we were together and they'll
never give you a massage the way I
did while talking about the weather

They'll never kiss your forehead
softly and stare deep into the eternity
of your eyes

But what they will do is tell you about
how they'll destroy what's between
your thighs and you'll moan, and
you'll fake and you'll tell them that
they are the shit

When deep down inside you'll wish it
was me because I didn't come here to
talk a good game

I didn't come here to tell you what I
can do I came here to remove all
doubt as well as memories of the old
school because my tongue knows no
bounds

I'm not here to imprint on your
mental

I'm here to leave soulful bruises on
you

Now let me ask, is this something you
think you can handle?

Sweats Lead to Sex

You know what you doing...
Yeah I see that print
Walking around in that male lingerie
Clearly, I was in denial about
how you hanging
It's on soft but damn sure hard not to
stare

Fuck it

I'm guilty
Reckless eyeballing
Yeah, I did it
Lock me up
Repeat offender
Cause I'm gone keep looking
I'm sorry if you're taken
Let Lil Mama know I'm not jockin
I'm just a woman
With a good eye for...fashion
I love the way the pockets provide
the perfect place to harbor that
fugitive
Peeking at me from underneath

those unmentionables
Making me moist
Teasing me with a good time
The drawstring grabbing the fabric

Gathering the thoughts in my mind
Creating an impression
of impure images

Damn these sweats
They're evil
They should be
reserved for the bedroom
The way they hang from your hips
And they stop right in that area that's
oh, so sexy
What do you call that
The area between the abs and the
pelvis
Fuck it
That dip
The term doesn't matter
It's the visual it provides
as it leads to the prize
A trail I love to follow
Got me wishing
I could be ya little secret

But for now...

I guess I'll keep it
Locked in my mind
My intuition doesn't lie
It's not an illusion
Ya shit is illuminated by them
got damn sweats
It's making me wet
I don't mean to protest
But as long as you wearing
this male lingerie
Please say less
Your lips haven't even separated
You spoke no words
Yet in my mind
My legs parted like a sew-in
Imagining my lips
wrapped tight around your tip
Sweats lead to sex
and I'm about to take off running
He has one eye on his victim and
I don't wanna be next

Ghetto Love

I need a real love
Like no other
Undeniable love
That kind I just can't get enough of

That I know we just went for hours
But I still need more of
what you serving

I can't keep my hands off you
Let me lift my skirt and snap
a pic of this pussy
Send it to you while you working
So, you know she's waiting
Type of love

Let's send the kids to grandma
for the weekend
Lock ourselves in the house
and workout
Sweating like a sauna
Take a shower
and create dejavu

I need a real love

That ghetto kinda love
You have to be ready to pump my gas

Spend some cash
And if I get outta line
Don't be afraid to smack my ass
Timid just won't do
Not if it's me you want to tame
You gotta beat it like Michael
Go on and on like Badu
And leave me feenin like Jodeci

If you can handle this love
Show me
Give me everything you got

Make me miss you
when I'm next to you
Crave you when you're already
Inside of me
Dream about you
And all the freaky shit you do

Love me hard, strong and
not too fast
Give me that Ghetto Love
and baby make it last

Warning

The stretching before the session
should have been a reflection
of his intentions
I missed the symbolism in his actions
Had I known I would have
taken a moment for a stretch or two,
incorporated some yoga,
maybe a quick prayer
Noticing my face during his
pre aerobic activity
He looked me in my eyes and said,
I meditated too
Silenced by the loud ass
foreshadowing in the room
I just smiled and said a quick
thank you
He just didn't know
I manifested his every move
Every thought, intention and
premeditated position
I had already claimed
for my next encounter
I needed this release
more than ever...

Death Row

Like a toddler in a kiddie pool
He didn't understand why
he had to get out

Mouthing the words "mine" he pouted
As I repeated last round,
you wearing me out

A gallon of water empty
And no sheets on the bed
He looked me in my eyes and had the
nerve to say, "baby,
let me give you some head."

My pearl throbbed
and betrayed my thoughts
Legs weak and cheeks sore,
I bit my lip and got on all fours

I had an agenda

Or so I thought...

I loved how he would grip my ass and
tease his tongue against my walls
Dip it in my ass while he dj'd my clit
But I knew where it would lead

And hopefully end...

He couldn't resist the temptation to
hit it in this position
Tossing and tasting like
the salad bar just opened

I released what he craved
and he moaned when
he caught my cream on his tongue

He swallowed and spoke slowly
"Baby...tasting your juice
is about to make me cum,
I need to feel you now and you
bet not run."

I laughed, arched my back more
and invited him in
Sliding in like it was the first time,
"Awww shit," slipped from his lips
He regained his focus and
tightened his grip

With his hands in the arch,
he held me still
"No running," he said
"Don't make me hold your head."

I moaned, "Yes, Daddy."
And held my position
Gripping him tighter than a white girl
with her first black piece
I rotated my hips and made sure
he felt all of me
I could feel him start throbbing
and getting close to release

I was ready to tap out
So, I said the magic words
"Let me feel you, Daddy. I'm ready
for you to paint these walls."

Barely audible he whispered,
"Yes, momma."

And sped up
Digging deep enough to let me know
I'd feel it two days later
I came again and it splashed
from his hips to his knees

Growling he gave me
just what I needed
He exploded and shot
baby bullets in me
Confirming she was his

But in case I missed it
He leaned down,
kissed my neck,
grinded one last time
And said...
Welcome to Death Row...

Temptation

I wanna fuck you like we're
 trying to stay warm
Plow through me like a
Minnesota winter

As if your main vessel is poisoned
And we have to Crank it
For the whole world to see

Let's release our inhibitions
Allow our alter egos to lead
In the club or the car
The world is ours
I wanna ride this wave until
we're seasick

I want the smell of my pussy to tickle
your nose hairs and temp
your taste buds
Causing a lump in your throat
Driving you insane at first lick

I'll follow your lead
As long as you direct me to ecstasy
Search my body for

the right response
Set off alarms in places
long untouched

Make me drift into dreams of
days that include you

While my stomach quivers
As I feel pressure in the
spots you lust

I need you not to hold back
Adrenaline rushing
Heart pumping
Sweat dripping
Bodies connecting

My lips moaning your name
Whispering between breathes
As the sound of your voice
penetrates my ears
Speaking on all the ways
I turn you on
How she's just as wet
as you dreamed
How you can't believe this

moment is finally here

You've lusted of this
exact position
Gripping my ass
With my legs wrapped tight

Digging until you hit
the perfect place

Providing the perfect amount of
pressure and pain

Written by: Souls InkPen

She had me...

Nervous as if I was first
learning to walk
yet I was seduced as if
called by her siren song

Her...gaze undressed me out of my
dickies, the stare in her eyes had me
feeling like I was about to lose my
virginity to the most beautiful angel
the Most High ever created and the
world had ever seen

I mean...

I was caught in a whirlwind,
a scene straight off the silver screen
and for a moment in time I was
contemplating crunching the value
betwixt our ages & phone numbers
to find whether the median and
mean averaged to how many times
I'd want her to cum for me

And no matter how many times I counted in that split second it always came to eternity

So, I did...

I flashed a smile, I walked by as if I was the dopest man in the room; I wanted her to understand by my mere presence I was trying to plant MY flag on HER moon

Trying to crash land my shuttle in her womb, wanting to take my battle to her bedroom but first, we would need to have a quick skirmish by the doorway leading to a chess match of mouths by the couch

Wait ... I would probably need to speak first before she walks out

"Are you gon be here for awhile?" Is the question I'll so eloquently choose,

Her response blissfully passes through my ears, piercing my soul, I just hope she's ready because I don't plan on leaving tonight, unless I'm leaving here with you.

Pressure

He had everything I desired
His walk was seduction for me

A simple gaze enough to
make my mouth water

It was rare
Probably one outta every hundred
But I couldn't deny when I saw it
B.D.E.
Big Dick Energy
The kind that made you lick your lips
and silently thank God
When your knees buckle and
your stomach drops
This roller-coaster feeling isn't about
the size of his...(you get it)
It's about the confidence in his stride
The look in his eyes
The way he speaks
Talks to your soul
Delivering the energy you need

He gave that and more
Before he even touched me
He applied pressure with his smile
Let his words slide down my spine

Tempted my taste buds
With each expressed thought

I salivated at the simplicity and
sincerity in his moves
Trying not to slip my panties
off too soon

I took a moment to listen...

To be continued...

Door Dash Energy

The sheets are wet
We're drenched in sweat
My pulse is racing
But we're not finished yet
I'm reaching for the walls
Like handlebars
And he's on my ass like
I shared my location
Delirious from his delivery
I asked his neighbors to help me
Ayudeme, Ayudeme
He laughed and said,
I'm dropping dick
off til the doorbell rings
I shed a tear for the pleasure
as well as the
unending sessions
In the back of my mind
wondering who was
paying us a visit
He never stopped
Like he had Red Bull in his veins
I came, he conquered
I came, he conquered

Punxsutawney Phil had to be
in the corner cheering him on
Round after round,
he reminded me why
he was daddy
His ability to handle my body
was beyond
normal rationality...
He knew what I needed by
the look in my eyes, before
my lips could concede it
I silently spoke of
the spots my body
needed him the most
He heard every request
and played no games
behind closed doors
This dick was making me lazy
I had already called in
Two days ago...

It started
And...
48 hours I'd been MIA
I'd promised him a meal
if he ate his appetizer
to satisfaction

My mouth watered
thinking about
the greens I bragged about
on my way to him

He slapped my cheeks and I couldn't
help but think
he deserved soul food
for his skills

But after this session
There would be
no homecooked meal
The doorbell rang
Simultaneously,
as we both came

Lethargic, legs limp
And craving more of him
But a break was needed
To catch my breath

I assumed the fetal position
With my ass facing the wall
Hopefully securing
a moment to myself
Kissing me, he said
let me go grab this food

I smiled and asked when
he ordered delivery

He kissed fat momma that time
and she purred like a kitten
Licking his lips, he said
While you were in the shower,
I knew you wouldn't have anything
but Door Dash Energy

Eroticism:

- sexual desire or excitement.

Wikipedia defines eroticism as:

Eroticism 'love, desire', and *-ism* is a quality that causes sexual feelings, as well as a philosophical contemplation concerning the aesthetics of sexual desire, sensuality, and romantic love. That quality may be found in any form of artwork, including painting, sculpture, photography, drama, film, music, or literature.

I encourage you to express your deepest desires in the safest way possible. Encounter the pleasure the universe created for you and release any restraints holding you back.
Happy writing...XOXO

Made in the USA
Coppell, TX
20 June 2026

81461792R00033